EMMANUEL JOSEPH

Command the Room, Command the Future, Public Speaking, Leadership, and the Power of Action

Copyright © 2025 by Emmanuel Joseph

All rights reserved. No part of this publication may be reproduced, stored or transmitted in any form or by any means, electronic, mechanical, photocopying, recording, scanning, or otherwise without written permission from the publisher. It is illegal to copy this book, post it to a website, or distribute it by any other means without permission.

First edition

*This book was professionally typeset on Reedsy.
Find out more at reedsy.com*

Contents

1	Chapter 1: The Power of Presence	1
2	Chapter 2: Crafting Compelling Narratives	3
3	Chapter 3: The Science of Persuasion	5
4	Chapter 4: Building Confidence and Overcoming Fear	7
5	Chapter 5: Non-Verbal Communication	9
6	Chapter 6: Mastering the Art of Delivery	11
7	Chapter 7: Engaging with Your Audience	13
8	Chapter 8: Handling Q&A Sessions with Grace	15
9	Chapter 9: Developing Your Unique Voice	17
10	Chapter 10: The Role of Emotional Intelligence	19
11	Chapter 11: Leading by Example	21
12	Chapter 12: The Power of Listening	23
13	Chapter 13: Building and Leading Teams	25
14	Chapter 14: Navigating Difficult Conversations	27
15	Chapter 15: The Future of Public Speaking	29
16	Chapter 16: Actionable Steps for Continuous Improvement	31

1

Chapter 1: The Power of Presence

In the grand theater of life, presence often separates the influential from the invisible. Cultivating a powerful presence is paramount for anyone looking to command a room and, ultimately, the future. But what does "presence" mean, and how can one harness it to leave a lasting impact?

Presence is an intangible aura that captivates and commands attention. It's an amalgamation of confidence, poise, and authenticity. When you walk into a room with a strong presence, you don't just take up space—you own it. This chapter delves into the essence of presence and its significance in public speaking and leadership.

Imagine you're in a crowded room filled with people, each vying for attention. The person who commands the room doesn't necessarily speak the loudest or boast the most impressive credentials. Instead, it's the individual who exudes an air of calm confidence, who listens intently and speaks with purpose. Their presence alone creates a sense of importance and draws people in. This magnetic quality is what we aim to cultivate in this chapter.

The first step in building presence is self-awareness. Understand your strengths, weaknesses, and unique qualities that set you apart. Embrace your authentic self, for authenticity is the cornerstone of presence. People are naturally drawn to those who are genuine and transparent. By being true to yourself, you create a sense of trust and credibility that resonates with others.

Next, we explore the importance of body language in establishing presence.

Non-verbal cues such as posture, eye contact, and facial expressions play a crucial role in how others perceive you. Stand tall, make direct eye contact, and smile genuinely. These small adjustments can significantly enhance your presence and make you more approachable and engaging.

Finally, we discuss the role of mindfulness and focus in cultivating presence. Being present in the moment, fully engaged and attentive, allows you to connect with others on a deeper level. Practice active listening, show empathy, and respond thoughtfully. By doing so, you create an environment where others feel valued and heard, further solidifying your presence.

Cultivating a powerful presence is a journey that requires continuous effort and self-reflection. As you hone this skill, you'll find that commanding the room becomes second nature, paving the way for you to command the future.

2

Chapter 2: Crafting Compelling Narratives

S torytelling is at the heart of effective public speaking. The ability to weave compelling narratives that captivate and inspire audiences is a vital skill for any leader. But what makes a story compelling, and how can you master the art of storytelling?

A compelling narrative goes beyond mere facts and figures; it evokes emotions and paints vivid pictures in the minds of the audience. The foundation of a great story is a clear and relatable message. Identify the core message you wish to convey and build your narrative around it. This message should resonate with your audience, addressing their needs, aspirations, or challenges.

One key element of storytelling is structure. A well-structured narrative has a clear beginning, middle, and end. The beginning sets the stage, introducing the characters and the context. The middle is where the plot thickens, presenting conflicts or challenges that need to be overcome. The end brings resolution, leaving the audience with a sense of closure and a memorable takeaway.

Another crucial aspect of storytelling is the use of vivid imagery and descriptive language. Paint a picture with your words, engaging the senses and emotions of your audience. Use metaphors, analogies, and anecdotes to make your story more relatable and impactful. Remember, a picture may be worth a thousand words, but a well-told story can leave an indelible mark on the hearts and minds of your listeners.

Lastly, we explore the importance of authenticity in storytelling. Share personal experiences and genuine emotions. Authenticity fosters connection and trust, making your narrative more believable and relatable. Don't be afraid to show vulnerability; it humanizes you and makes your message more compelling.

By mastering the art of crafting compelling narratives, you can captivate your audience, inspire action, and leave a lasting impact. Your stories become powerful tools that help you command the room and, ultimately, the future.

3

Chapter 3: The Science of Persuasion

Understanding the principles of persuasion is critical for leaders and speakers alike. Persuasion is not about manipulation; it's about guiding people toward a new perspective or action that benefits them and aligns with your message. This chapter examines the psychological aspects of persuasion and how to leverage them effectively.

At the heart of persuasion lies ethos, pathos, and logos—three modes of persuasion defined by Aristotle. Ethos refers to the credibility and character of the speaker. To persuade an audience, you must establish trust and demonstrate expertise in your subject matter. This can be achieved through clear communication, consistency, and authenticity. Your audience is more likely to be persuaded if they believe in you and your message.

Pathos is the emotional appeal. Emotions are powerful drivers of human behavior, and tapping into your audience's emotions can significantly enhance your persuasive efforts. Share personal stories, use vivid language, and create a sense of urgency. By connecting emotionally with your audience, you make your message more relatable and impactful.

Logos is the logical appeal. This involves presenting clear, rational arguments supported by evidence and data. Use facts, statistics, and logical reasoning to build a compelling case for your message. When your audience sees that your arguments are well-founded and logical, they are more likely to be persuaded.

Another crucial aspect of persuasion is understanding your audience's needs, values, and motivations. Tailor your message to resonate with their interests and address their concerns. By showing empathy and understanding, you create a sense of alignment and make your audience more receptive to your message.

Additionally, we explore the role of social proof in persuasion. People are influenced by the actions and opinions of others. Highlight testimonials, endorsements, and case studies to demonstrate that others have benefited from your message or product. This builds credibility and encourages your audience to follow suit.

Finally, we discuss the importance of consistency and repetition in persuasion. Repeated exposure to a message increases familiarity and acceptance. Reinforce your key points throughout your speech and provide consistent messaging across different platforms and interactions.

By mastering the science of persuasion, you can effectively influence opinions, drive action, and command any room with confidence and clarity.

4

Chapter 4: Building Confidence and Overcoming Fear

Confidence is the cornerstone of commanding any room. However, the fear of public speaking is one of the most common and debilitating fears people face. This chapter provides practical techniques to build unshakeable confidence and conquer the fear of public speaking.

Firstly, preparation is key. The more prepared you are, the more confident you will feel. Research your topic thoroughly, organize your thoughts, and practice your speech multiple times. Familiarity with your content reduces anxiety and boosts confidence. Consider practicing in front of a mirror, recording yourself, or rehearsing in front of a trusted friend or family member.

Visualization is another powerful tool for building confidence. Visualize yourself giving a successful speech, commanding the room, and receiving positive feedback. This mental rehearsal helps condition your mind for success and reduces anxiety. Positive affirmations and self-talk can also boost your confidence. Remind yourself of your strengths, achievements, and the value you bring to your audience.

Breathing exercises and relaxation techniques can help calm your nerves before and during your speech. Deep breathing, progressive muscle relaxation, and mindfulness practices can reduce physical symptoms of anxiety and help you stay focused and composed.

Another technique is to reframe your perspective on public speaking. Instead of viewing it as a daunting task, see it as an opportunity to share your knowledge and connect with others. Focus on the value you provide to your audience rather than worrying about their judgment. This shift in mindset can reduce anxiety and enhance your confidence.

Engaging with your audience can also boost your confidence. Establish eye contact, smile, and interact with your listeners. Positive feedback and engagement from your audience can reinforce your confidence and make the experience more enjoyable.

Finally, embrace imperfections and learn from experiences. Mistakes and setbacks are a natural part of the learning process. Instead of dwelling on them, use them as opportunities for growth and improvement. Over time, you will build resilience and confidence in your public speaking abilities.

By implementing these techniques, you can build unshakeable confidence, overcome the fear of public speaking, and command any room with ease.

5

Chapter 5: Non-Verbal Communication

Often, what you don't say speaks louder than words. Non-verbal communication, including body language, facial expressions, and gestures, plays a crucial role in reinforcing your message and establishing a connection with your audience. This chapter explores the power of non-verbal communication and how to harness it effectively.

Body language is a powerful tool for conveying confidence and credibility. Stand tall with good posture, as it exudes confidence and authority. Avoid slouching or crossing your arms, as these can signal defensiveness or insecurity. Use open and expansive gestures to engage your audience and emphasize key points.

Eye contact is another essential element of non-verbal communication. Making direct eye contact with your audience helps establish a connection and builds trust. It shows that you are attentive and engaged. However, be mindful not to stare or make prolonged eye contact, as it can be uncomfortable. Instead, practice scanning the room and making brief eye contact with different individuals.

Facial expressions convey a range of emotions and can significantly impact how your message is received. Smile genuinely to create a warm and approachable demeanor. Use appropriate facial expressions to match the tone and content of your speech. For example, show enthusiasm when discussing exciting ideas or concern when addressing challenges. Your facial expressions should align with your words to reinforce your message.

Gestures and movement can enhance your delivery and keep your audience engaged. Use purposeful gestures to emphasize key points and add dynamism to your presentation. Avoid repetitive or distracting movements, such as fidgeting or pacing. Instead, use natural and controlled gestures that complement your message. Moving around the stage or room can also help maintain audience interest and create a sense of energy.

Finally, we explore the importance of congruence in non-verbal communication. Your words and actions should align to create a consistent and believable message. Incongruence between verbal and non-verbal cues can lead to confusion and mistrust. Be mindful of your body language, facial expressions, and gestures to ensure they reinforce and support your message.

By mastering non-verbal communication, you can enhance your presence, build trust, and create a powerful connection with your audience. This skill is essential for commanding any room and delivering impactful presentations.

6

Chapter 6: Mastering the Art of Delivery

The delivery of a speech can significantly influence its impact. Regardless of how compelling your content is, if it's not delivered effectively, it may fail to resonate with your audience. In this chapter, we discuss pacing, tone, and vocal variety, providing tips to keep your audience engaged and your message impactful.

Pacing refers to the speed at which you speak. Speaking too quickly can cause your audience to miss important points, while speaking too slowly may lead to boredom and disengagement. Find a balanced pace that allows you to articulate your message clearly while maintaining the audience's interest. Vary your pacing to emphasize key points and maintain dynamism in your delivery. For example, slow down when making a crucial statement to allow it to sink in and speed up during less critical parts to maintain momentum.

Tone of voice conveys your emotions and attitude towards the subject matter. A monotone delivery can be dull and uninspiring, while a dynamic tone can evoke emotions and captivate your audience. Adjust your tone to match the content of your speech. Show enthusiasm when discussing exciting ideas, seriousness when addressing important issues, and empathy when discussing sensitive topics. Your tone should reflect the message you want to convey and the emotions you wish to evoke in your audience.

Vocal variety involves changing your pitch, volume, and rhythm to create interest and maintain engagement. Varying your pitch can emphasize different parts of your speech and convey different emotions. Raising your pitch can indicate excitement or urgency, while lowering it can signal seriousness or authority. Adjusting your volume can also enhance your delivery. Speak louder when you want to emphasize a point and softer to create intimacy or draw attention. Rhythm, or the natural flow of your speech, can be varied by using pauses effectively. Pauses can add dramatic effect, allow the audience to process information, and give you a moment to collect your thoughts.

Practicing your delivery is crucial for mastering these techniques. Record yourself, listen to playback, and make adjustments as needed. Practice in front of a mirror to observe your facial expressions and body language. Seek feedback from trusted friends or colleagues and make improvements based on their observations. The more you practice, the more comfortable and confident you will become in your delivery.

By mastering the art of delivery, you can ensure that your message is impactful, engaging, and memorable. This skill is essential for commanding any room and making a lasting impression on your audience.

7

Chapter 7: Engaging with Your Audience

An engaged audience is a responsive audience. Creating a dynamic interaction with your audience ensures they are invested in your message and more likely to take action. This chapter explores strategies to engage your audience effectively.

One key strategy is to start with a strong opening. Capture your audience's attention from the beginning with a powerful quote, a surprising fact, or a thought-provoking question. An engaging opening sets the tone for your speech and encourages your audience to listen attentively.

Interactive elements can also enhance audience engagement. Encourage participation through questions, polls, or activities. Ask open-ended questions that prompt your audience to think and respond. Incorporate polls or surveys to gather their opinions and make them feel involved. Interactive activities, such as group discussions or exercises, can break the monotony and keep your audience engaged.

Using storytelling to illustrate your points can also create a connection with your audience. Share personal anecdotes, case studies, or hypothetical scenarios that relate to your message. Stories evoke emotions and make your content more relatable and memorable. Ensure your stories are relevant to your audience and support your key points.

Visual aids, such as slides, videos, or props, can enhance your presentation and keep your audience engaged. Use visuals to highlight important information, provide context, or add interest to your speech. Ensure your visuals are clear, relevant, and not overwhelming. They should complement your message, not distract from it.

Another strategy is to maintain eye contact and use body language effectively. Making eye contact with different individuals creates a sense of connection and shows that you are engaged with your audience. Use open and expressive body language to convey confidence and enthusiasm. Your body language should align with your message and reinforce your words.

Finally, be responsive to your audience's feedback and adapt as needed. Pay attention to their reactions and adjust your delivery accordingly. If you notice signs of boredom or confusion, change your pace, tone, or approach to re-engage them. Being flexible and responsive shows that you value your audience and are attuned to their needs.

By employing these strategies, you can create a dynamic interaction with your audience, ensuring they are engaged and invested in your message. Engaging your audience is key to commanding any room and driving action.

8

Chapter 8: Handling Q&A Sessions with Grace

Q&A sessions can be unpredictable and daunting, but they are an excellent opportunity to further connect with your audience and reinforce your message. This chapter provides strategies to handle questions with poise and clarity, maintaining control and credibility throughout.

First, prepare for potential questions in advance. Anticipate the types of questions your audience may ask and prepare thoughtful responses. This preparation allows you to handle questions confidently and reduces the likelihood of being caught off guard. Consider practicing with a friend or colleague who can pose challenging questions to simulate the experience.

During the Q&A session, listen carefully to each question. Show respect and attentiveness by maintaining eye contact and not interrupting. Paraphrase the question to ensure you understand it correctly and to give yourself a moment to gather your thoughts. This also shows the audience that you are actively listening and engaged.

Respond to questions with clarity and conciseness. Provide straightforward answers and avoid unnecessary jargon or lengthy explanations. If you don't know the answer to a question, be honest and acknowledge it. Offer to follow up with the information later or direct the question to a relevant source.

Honesty and transparency build credibility and trust with your audience.

Stay composed and confident, even when faced with difficult or hostile questions. Maintain a calm and respectful demeanor, and avoid becoming defensive or confrontational. Address the question thoughtfully and redirect the focus back to your main message if necessary. By staying composed, you demonstrate professionalism and control.

Encourage other audience members to ask questions by creating a welcoming environment. Use phrases like "That's a great question," or "Thank you for bringing that up," to show appreciation for their participation. This encourages more engagement and fosters a positive interaction.

Finally, manage the time effectively during the Q&A session. Set clear guidelines for the duration and the number of questions to ensure the session stays on track. Politely wrap up the session by thanking the audience for their questions and reiterating key points from your speech.

By employing these strategies, you can handle Q&A sessions with grace, maintain control, and reinforce your message. Effective Q&A sessions enhance your credibility and leave a positive impression on your audience.

9

Chapter 9: Developing Your Unique Voice

Your unique voice is your greatest asset in public speaking. It sets you apart and makes your presentations memorable and genuine. This chapter helps you discover and cultivate your authentic speaking style.

Discovering your unique voice begins with self-awareness. Reflect on your strengths, passions, and experiences. What topics excite you? What personal stories or insights can you share? Embrace your individuality and let your personality shine through in your speeches. Authenticity is key to connecting with your audience and building trust.

Experiment with different styles and techniques to find what resonates with you. Practice speaking in different tones, pacing, and gestures to see what feels natural and effective. Seek feedback from trusted friends or colleagues and make adjustments based on their observations. The more you experiment, the closer you get to discovering your unique voice.

Consistency is essential in developing your unique voice. Maintain a consistent tone and style across different speeches and platforms. This consistency builds your brand and makes you recognizable to your audience. However, be adaptable and flexible to different contexts and audiences. Tailor your message and delivery to suit the specific needs and expectations of your audience while staying true to your core style.

Authenticity involves being honest and transparent with your audience.

Share personal stories, experiences, and insights that reflect your true self. Vulnerability can be powerful and relatable. Don't be afraid to show your emotions and imperfections; they humanize you and make your message more compelling.

Finally, embrace continuous improvement. Public speaking is a journey, and there is always room for growth. Seek opportunities to refine your skills, learn from other speakers, and stay updated with trends and best practices. Embrace feedback and use it as a tool for growth. The more you practice and learn, the more refined and authentic your unique voice becomes.

By developing your unique voice, you can create memorable and impactful presentations that resonate with your audience. Your voice is your greatest asset in commanding any room and leaving a lasting impression.

10

Chapter 10: The Role of Emotional Intelligence

Emotional intelligence (EI) plays a crucial role in effective leadership and public speaking. EI involves the ability to recognize, understand, and manage our own emotions, as well as the emotions of others. This chapter explores the components of emotional intelligence and how to apply them in various contexts.

Emotional intelligence is comprised of five key components: self-awareness, self-regulation, motivation, empathy, and social skills. Each of these components contributes to a leader's ability to connect with others, make informed decisions, and inspire action.

Self-awareness is the foundation of emotional intelligence. It involves understanding your emotions, strengths, weaknesses, and values. By being self-aware, you can recognize how your emotions impact your thoughts and behaviors. This awareness allows you to manage your emotions effectively and respond to situations with clarity and composure. Practice self-reflection and seek feedback from others to enhance your self-awareness.

Self-regulation is the ability to control and manage your emotions. It involves staying calm and composed under pressure, avoiding impulsive reactions, and adapting to changing circumstances. Self-regulation allows you to maintain control and make thoughtful decisions, even in challenging situations. Techniques such as deep breathing, mindfulness, and stress management can help improve self-regulation.

Motivation is the drive to achieve goals and pursue success. Emotionally intelligent leaders are intrinsically motivated and have a passion for their work. They set high standards for themselves and others, and they are committed to continuous improvement. Cultivate a growth mindset and stay focused on your goals to enhance your motivation.

Empathy is the ability to understand and share the feelings of others. It involves recognizing and appreciating different perspectives and emotions. Empathy allows you to build strong relationships, foster collaboration, and create a supportive environment. Practice active listening, show genuine concern for others, and seek to understand their viewpoints to enhance your empathy.

Social skills are the abilities to interact and communicate effectively with others. Emotionally intelligent leaders are skilled in building and maintaining relationships, resolving conflicts, and inspiring others. They use effective communication, persuasion, and influence to achieve their goals. Develop strong interpersonal skills, practice effective communication, and build rapport with others to enhance your social skills.

By cultivating emotional intelligence, you can enhance your leadership and public speaking abilities. EI allows you to connect with others on a deeper level, make informed decisions, and inspire action. It is a vital skill for commanding any room and leading with impact.

11

Chapter 11: Leading by Example

Leadership is not just about words; it's about actions. Leading by example is a powerful way to inspire others and create a culture of integrity and authenticity. This chapter discusses the importance of leading by example and the impact of integrity and authenticity in leadership.

Leading by example involves demonstrating the behaviors and values you expect from others. As a leader, your actions set the tone for your team or organization. When you lead by example, you build trust and credibility, and you create a positive and inspiring environment.

Integrity is a core component of leading by example. It involves being honest, ethical, and consistent in your actions. Leaders with integrity are transparent and accountable, and they uphold high standards of behavior. By demonstrating integrity, you create a culture of trust and respect, and you encourage others to follow your example.

Authenticity is another crucial aspect of leading by example. It involves being genuine and true to yourself. Authentic leaders are open and honest about their strengths, weaknesses, and values. They are not afraid to show vulnerability and admit mistakes. By being authentic, you create a sense of relatability and connection with others, and you inspire them to be their true selves.

Consistency is key to leading by example. Your actions should align with your words, and you should demonstrate the same values and behaviors consistently. Inconsistencies can lead to confusion and mistrust. By being consistent, you create a sense of stability and reliability, and you reinforce the values and behaviors you want to see in others.

Leading by example also involves taking responsibility and being accountable for your actions. When you make a mistake, acknowledge it and take steps to rectify it. By taking responsibility, you demonstrate humility and a commitment to continuous improvement. This sets a positive example for others and encourages a culture of accountability.

By leading by example, you can inspire others, build trust, and create a positive and authentic environment. Your actions speak louder than words, and they have a lasting impact on those around you.

12

Chapter 12: The Power of Listening

Listening is an often-overlooked skill in public speaking and leadership. Effective listening enhances your ability to connect with others, build relationships, and make informed decisions. This chapter emphasizes the importance of active listening and how it enhances your ability to connect and lead.

Active listening involves fully engaging with the speaker, understanding their message, and responding thoughtfully. It requires focused attention, empathy, and an open mind. Active listening goes beyond hearing words; it involves understanding the emotions and intentions behind the words.

One key aspect of active listening is giving your full attention to the speaker. Eliminate distractions, make eye contact, and show genuine interest in their message. Avoid interrupting or thinking about your response while they are speaking. By giving your full attention, you show respect and create a sense of connection.

Empathy is another crucial element of active listening. Put yourself in the speaker's shoes and try to understand their perspective and emotions. Show empathy by acknowledging their feelings and responding with understanding and compassion. Empathetic listening creates a supportive environment and fosters trust and rapport.

Ask open-ended questions to encourage the speaker to elaborate on their thoughts and feelings. Open-ended questions invite deeper conversation and demonstrate your interest in understanding their perspective. Avoid closed-ended questions that can be answered with a simple "yes" or "no."

Reflect and paraphrase the speaker's message to ensure you understand it correctly. Reflecting involves repeating the speaker's words in your own words, while paraphrasing involves summarizing their message. This demonstrates that you are actively engaged and allows for clarification if needed.

Provide feedback and responses that show you are listening and engaged. Feedback can be verbal, such as affirming statements or questions, or non-verbal, such as nodding or smiling. Responsive listening creates a dynamic interaction and encourages open communication.

Finally, practice patience and avoid rushing the conversation. Allow the speaker to express their thoughts fully and take their time. Patience shows respect and creates a comfortable environment for open dialogue.

By mastering the power of listening, you can enhance your ability to connect with others, build strong relationships, and make informed decisions. Listening is a vital skill for effective leadership and public speaking, and it plays a crucial role in commanding any room.

13

Chapter 13: Building and Leading Teams

Effective leadership often involves building and leading teams. A successful team is greater than the sum of its parts, and a strong leader knows how to harness the strengths of each team member to achieve collective goals. This chapter provides insights into team dynamics, fostering collaboration, and inspiring collective action.

Building a cohesive team begins with selecting the right members. Choose individuals with diverse skills, perspectives, and experiences that complement each other. A well-rounded team brings a variety of strengths to the table and can tackle challenges from different angles. Ensure that each team member understands their role and how it contributes to the overall goals.

Fostering a positive team culture is essential for collaboration and success. Create an environment of trust, respect, and open communication. Encourage team members to share their ideas, opinions, and feedback. Show appreciation for their contributions and recognize their achievements. A positive culture motivates team members and enhances their commitment to the team's goals.

Effective communication is the cornerstone of team collaboration. Ensure that communication is clear, transparent, and consistent. Use regular team meetings, updates, and feedback sessions to keep everyone informed and aligned. Encourage active listening and open dialogue to address any issues or concerns promptly.

Empower team members by giving them autonomy and responsibility. Trust them to make decisions and take ownership of their tasks. Empowerment fosters a sense of accountability and initiative, and it allows team members to showcase their strengths and creativity. Provide support and guidance, but avoid micromanaging.

Lead by example and demonstrate the behaviors and values you expect from your team. Show integrity, authenticity, and commitment to the team's goals. Your actions set the tone for the team and inspire them to follow your lead. Be approachable and accessible, and provide support and mentorship when needed.

Encourage collaboration and teamwork by promoting a sense of unity and shared purpose. Foster a collaborative environment where team members can work together, share knowledge, and support each other. Use team-building activities and exercises to strengthen relationships and build trust.

Finally, inspire collective action by setting clear goals, providing a vision, and motivating the team. Communicate the bigger picture and the impact of their contributions. Inspire enthusiasm and passion for the team's goals, and celebrate successes along the way. A motivated and inspired team is more likely to achieve collective success.

By building and leading strong teams, you can harness the power of collaboration and achieve remarkable results. Effective team leadership is essential for commanding any room and driving collective action.

14

Chapter 14: Navigating Difficult Conversations

Difficult conversations are inevitable in leadership. Whether addressing performance issues, delivering bad news, or handling conflicts, the ability to navigate these conversations with empathy and effectiveness is crucial. This chapter explores strategies to handle difficult conversations while maintaining relationships and achieving resolutions.

The first step in navigating difficult conversations is preparation. Understand the context and the underlying issues before initiating the conversation. Gather relevant information, consider different perspectives, and anticipate potential reactions. Preparation allows you to approach the conversation with clarity and confidence.

Choose an appropriate time and place for the conversation. Ensure privacy and minimize distractions to create a comfortable environment. Timing is also important; avoid having difficult conversations when emotions are high or when either party is under significant stress. A conducive setting fosters open and constructive dialogue.

Start the conversation with empathy and respect. Acknowledge the other person's feelings and perspective. Use "I" statements to express your concerns without blaming or accusing. For example, say "I noticed that…" instead of "You always…" This approach creates a non-threatening environment and encourages openness.

Active listening is crucial in difficult conversations. Give the other person your full attention, avoid interrupting, and show genuine interest in their perspective. Reflect and paraphrase their statements to ensure understanding. Empathetic listening demonstrates respect and fosters mutual understanding.

Stay calm and composed throughout the conversation. Manage your emotions and avoid becoming defensive or confrontational. Use deep breathing and other relaxation techniques to maintain control. A calm demeanor helps de-escalate tension and keeps the conversation focused on finding solutions.

Focus on the issue at hand and avoid personal attacks or bringing up unrelated matters. Stay solution-oriented and work collaboratively to identify potential resolutions. Encourage the other person to share their ideas and perspectives. By involving them in the problem-solving process, you foster a sense of ownership and commitment to the resolution.

End the conversation on a positive note. Summarize the key points discussed, reiterate any agreements or action items, and express appreciation for the other person's willingness to engage in the conversation. A positive conclusion reinforces a sense of respect and collaboration.

By employing these strategies, you can navigate difficult conversations with empathy and effectiveness, maintaining relationships and achieving resolutions. This skill is essential for effective leadership and creating a positive and productive environment.

15

Chapter 15: The Future of Public Speaking

Public speaking is evolving with technology and societal changes. As we look to the future, it is essential to adapt and stay relevant. This chapter examines emerging trends in public speaking and how to leverage them to stay effective.

One significant trend is the rise of virtual and hybrid presentations. With advancements in technology, public speaking is no longer confined to physical spaces. Virtual platforms and hybrid events have become common, allowing speakers to reach wider audiences. Mastering virtual communication skills, such as using video conferencing tools, engaging remote audiences, and managing technical aspects, is crucial for future success.

Interactive and immersive experiences are also shaping the future of public speaking. Audience engagement is enhanced through interactive elements like live polls, Q&A sessions, and virtual reality (VR) experiences. These tools create a dynamic and participatory environment, making presentations more engaging and memorable.

Data-driven presentations are becoming increasingly important. Incorporating data and analytics into your presentations adds credibility and supports your message. Use visual aids, infographics, and data visualizations to present complex information in a clear and compelling manner. Staying informed about data trends and leveraging data effectively will be essential for future public speakers.

Another emerging trend is the emphasis on inclusivity and diversity in public speaking. Audiences are becoming more diverse, and it is important to be mindful of different perspectives and cultural sensitivities. Use inclusive language, acknowledge diverse viewpoints, and create an environment where everyone feels valued and respected. Inclusivity enhances connection and broadens the impact of your message.

Continuous learning and adaptability are crucial for staying relevant in the future. Public speaking skills are constantly evolving, and it is essential to stay updated with new techniques, tools, and best practices. Seek opportunities for professional development, attend workshops and conferences, and learn from other speakers. Embrace change and be willing to adapt to new trends and technologies.

By understanding and leveraging these emerging trends, you can stay relevant and effective in the future of public speaking. Adapting to change and continuously improving your skills will ensure you command any room, whether physical or virtual.

16

Chapter 16: Actionable Steps for Continuous Improvement

Mastery in public speaking and leadership is a continuous journey. There is always room for growth, and taking actionable steps for continuous improvement is essential. This chapter provides practical strategies and resources for ongoing development.

Set specific goals for your improvement. Identify areas where you want to grow, such as enhancing your delivery, refining your storytelling, or building your confidence. Setting clear and measurable goals provides direction and motivation for your improvement journey.

Seek feedback regularly. Feedback from trusted friends, colleagues, or mentors provides valuable insights into your strengths and areas for improvement. Actively seek feedback after presentations and use it constructively to make necessary adjustments. Be open to criticism and view it as an opportunity for growth.

Practice consistently. Regular practice is key to honing your skills and building confidence. Practice speaking in front of a mirror, record yourself, or rehearse with a trusted friend. Join public speaking clubs or groups, such as Toastmasters, to gain more practice opportunities and receive structured feedback.

Stay updated with trends and best practices. Attend workshops, seminars, and conferences on public speaking and leadership. Read books, articles, and research papers to stay informed about new techniques and insights. Continuous learning keeps you updated with the latest developments and helps you stay ahead.

Observe and learn from other speakers. Watch TED Talks, keynote speeches, and presentations by renowned speakers. Pay attention to their delivery, style, and techniques. Analyze what makes their speeches effective and incorporate those elements into your own presentations.

Engage in self-reflection. Regularly reflect on your performances and experiences. Identify what worked well and what could be improved. Keep a journal to track your progress, set new goals, and document your learnings. Self-reflection fosters self-awareness and helps you identify patterns and areas for growth.

Utilize resources and tools for improvement. There are numerous resources available, such as online courses, books, and apps, that can help you enhance your public speaking and leadership skills. Take advantage of these resources to supplement your learning and practice.

Finally, embrace a growth mindset. Understand that mastery is a continuous journey, and setbacks are part of the process. Stay committed to your improvement and view challenges as opportunities to learn and grow. A growth mindset fosters resilience, motivation, and a positive attitude toward continuous improvement.

By taking actionable steps for continuous improvement, you can enhance your public speaking and leadership abilities. Continuous growth ensures that you stay effective, relevant, and confident in commanding any room.

Conclusion: Commanding the Future

We have explored the journey of mastering public speaking, leadership, and the power of action. The skills and strategies discussed in this book are essential for commanding the room and, ultimately, commanding the future. By cultivating presence, crafting compelling narratives, understanding persuasion, building confidence, mastering non-verbal communication, delivering impactful speeches, engaging with audiences, handling Q&A sessions, developing your unique voice, leveraging emotional intelligence,

CHAPTER 16: ACTIONABLE STEPS FOR CONTINUOUS IMPROVEMENT

leading by example, practicing active listening, building and leading teams, navigating difficult conversations, adapting to future trends, and continuously improving, you can become a powerful and influential speaker and leader.

As you apply these lessons, remember that mastery is a continuous journey. Embrace growth, stay adaptable, and remain committed to your development. By doing so, you will command your future with confidence, inspire others, and make a lasting impact.

In **"Command the Room, Command the Future: Public Speaking, Leadership, and the Power of Action**," you'll embark on a transformative journey to master the art of public speaking and leadership. This book delves into the essential skills and strategies needed to captivate audiences, inspire action, and lead with confidence.

You'll learn how to cultivate a powerful presence, craft compelling narratives, and understand the science of persuasion. Discover practical techniques to build unshakeable confidence, master non-verbal communication, and deliver impactful speeches. Engage with your audience effectively, handle Q&A sessions with grace, and develop your unique voice to stand out.

The book also explores the role of emotional intelligence in leadership, the importance of leading by example, and the power of active listening. Gain insights into building and leading strong teams, navigating difficult conversations, and adapting to future trends in public speaking.

With actionable steps for continuous improvement, this book provides a comprehensive guide to becoming a powerful and influential speaker and leader. Command the room, command the future, and embrace the power of action.

www.ingramcontent.com/pod-product-compliance
Lightning Source LLC
LaVergne TN
LVHW010442070526
838199LV00066B/6146